天涯客詩選

吳江宋哲生著

文史哲出版社印行

國家圖書館出版品預行編目資料

天涯客詩選 / 宋哲生著. -- 初版. --臺北市：文
史哲,民 91
　　面；　公分
　　ISBN 957-549-428-8 (平裝)

　1.

851.486　　　　　　　　　　　　　91006174

天 涯 客 詩 選

著　　　者：宋　　　哲　　　生
出 版 者：文 史 哲 出 版 社
http://www.lapen.com.tw
登記證字號：行政院新聞局版臺業字五三三七號
發 行 人：彭　　　正　　　雄
發 行 所：文 史 哲 出 版 社
印 刷 者：文 史 哲 出 版 社
臺北市羅斯福路一段七十二巷四號
郵政劃撥帳號：一六一八○一七五
電話 886-2-23511028・傳真 886-2-23965656

實價新臺幣一○○元

中 華 民 國 九 十 一 年 (2002) 四 月 初 版

天涯客詩選

目　錄

詩序：生命之歌

生命猶如燭一枝　　臨風閃鑠幾多時
縱能散發光和熱　　轉瞬煙消不久持

生命猶如白色箋　　塗紅著綠任君填
何須濃抹招人眼　　淡寫輕描分外妍

生命猶如酒一杯　　與人歡樂與人哀
每當細品杯中味　　苦到盡頭甘始來

生命猶如一粒沙　　隨波逐浪闖天涯
奈何身在洪濤裏　　空有壯懷付浪花

生命猶如一朵花　　含苞初放競相誇
一朝凋謝無人問　　且待春來再發芽

生命猶如夢一場　　貧窮富貴盡黃粱
但能看破名和利　　夢裏乾坤處處香

一、萍蹤散紀

西安行

謁黃帝陵

尋根行陝北　千里謁黃陵
浪作天涯客　常懷故國心
思源情戚戚　繞墓柏森森
民族英魂在　精神貫古今

註：黃帝陵在陝西　黃陵縣之橋山，古柏參
　　天，氣象肅穆。

謁秦始皇陵

鬱鬱驪山草　長眠秦始皇
焚書坑異己　爭霸滅強梁
陶俑千年現　邊城萬里張
中華成一統　功過細評量

註：秦始皇陵在陝西臨潼縣驪山之麓。自
　　1974年起，在陵墓東側，發現兵馬俑
　　坑，埋有數千具真人大小之陶製彩繪
　　兵馬俑，排隊列陣，展現軍容。

登大雁塔

登塔縱雙眸	河山眼底收
經文傳後世	帝業剩荒丘
古道添新綠	夕陽照舊州
人生嗟苦短	天地自悠悠

註：大雁塔在西安市南郊慈恩寺內，建於
　　公元 652 年，當時主持僧玄奘為保護
　　從印度取回之經籍，由唐高宗資助，
　　在寺內西院修建，作為藏經之所。

北京紀遊

飛北京

海峽風雲未見晴　　中原遙望不通行
江湖倦鳥歸心急　　繞道澳門飛北京

經澳門

澳門好似孤兒島　　異族經營成賭堡
今日重投慈母懷　　歸宗認祖焚香禱

天安門

門內有城門外牆　　天安氣勢不尋常
改朝換代門前演　　總是登場又下場

清故宮

宮殿深沉似廟堂　　庭園花木幾滄桑
雕闌玉砌今猶在　　紅袖朱顏已早亡

頤和園

頤園勝景美無儔　　北海風光眼底收
外寇入侵無力抗　　只緣戰艦變龍舟

註：慈禧移用巨額軍費，建設頤和園，致無力抗禦外侮，
　　招來八國聯軍之辱。

恭王府

和珅豪宅勝君王　一代巨貪天下揚
享盡榮華終自毀　白綾三尺掛高梁

註：恭王府原為乾隆寵臣和珅之豪華私宅。和珅恃寵貪
　　污，生活奢侈糜爛，後為嘉慶帝賜死，財產全部沒
　　收，其豪宅成為恭親王之王府。

皇帝宴

不若君王坐九重　我登龍椅甚輕鬆
民間疾苦毋須問　只望樽中酒正濃

註：北海仿膳飯店，擺皇帝宴，設有龍椅，供遊客一過
　　皇帝之癮。

紅樓宴

大觀園內紅樓宴　賈府排場今得見
各色珍饈有美稱　嘗來樣樣難吞嚥

註：大觀樓酒家設紅樓宴，完全依照「紅樓夢」小說中
　　描述製作，提供清代風味之筵席，菜單雖美，甚難
　　下嚥。

長　城

蜿蜒山嶽一條龍　拱衛邊疆挫敵鋒
首尾挺伸超萬里　月球遙望見真容

註：太空人阿姆斯壯登陸月球後曾云：「長城為地球上唯
　　一之人工建築物，能從月球看到。」

姑蘇之旅

虎丘塔（建於公元 969 年）

閱盡滄桑看虎丘　　千年古塔鎮山頭
歷朝多少興亡事　　卻似雲煙過眼收

劍池（吳王闔閭陵墓所在地）

峭壁圍池倒影浮　　春秋遺蹟至今留
吳王殉葬三千劍　　日引萬人到此遊

劍池試劍石

試劍石前一劍橫　　不由豪氣膽邊生
若非鬢髮斑斑白　　定走江湖掃不平

虎丘雲岩寺（大雄寶殿擊鼓）

佛祖悠閒坐殿中　　忽聽殿外鼓聲隆
何人敢把佛堂闖　　來了江南老頑童

訪寒山寺

姑蘇名剎寒山寺　　墨客騷人結伴來
歌頌詩僧聲不斷　　寒山拾得笑顏開

寒山寺（與唐詩人張繼銅像合影）

楓橋名句爭傳誦　　古剎鐘聲激共鳴
我亦騷壇流浪客　　得瞻風采慰平生

寒山寺鐘樓

夜泊楓橋入夢中　　寒山寺裡響叮咚
只因張繼曾吟唱　　天下聞名一口鐘

楓橋遠眺

獨上楓橋望四週　　鐵鈴關口對橋頭
江楓漁火均難覓　　遊艇二三水上浮

拙政園賞荷

艷紅翠綠鬥芬芳　　出水荷花開滿塘
小坐池傍心欲醉　　猶如身在美人鄉

登靈岩山（位於蘇州西南，多奇石故名靈岩）

手扶禪杖上山巔　　斜倚靈岩枕石眠
仰望長空心坦蕩　　一生無愧對蒼天

靈岩山寺進香

滿懷懺悔上靈岩　　無奈離鄉數十寒
今日歸來還宿願　　焚香默禱報平安

蘇州運河

上通冀魯下蘇杭　　船滿運河日夜航
我欲乘槎浮水去　　不知今夕宿何方

中歐之旅

詩人會布城

寰宇騷人聚一堂　　撚鬚搔首索詩腸
吟來警句傳千古　　譜出佳音娛四方
齊唱和平驅戾氣　　互通心曲飲瓊漿
布城雅集空前事　　多瑙河邊萬丈光

註：第十八屆世界詩人大會於 1998 年 8 月 19 日至 23 日
　　在斯洛伐克首都布拉德斯拉瓦(Bratislava)召開。會
　　場即在多瑙河邊的多瑙河飯店(Hotel Danube)。

布拉德斯拉瓦(Bratislava)

莫道布城宮殿多　　帝王氣象有餘波
當年歌舞昇平日　　音樂悠揚倩影娑

註：布拉德斯拉瓦為前匈牙利王朝之首都，長達三百年，
　　宮殿頗多，現為斯洛伐克政府首長辦公及宴會之所。

泛舟多瑙河

多瑙泛舟結伴遊　　乘風破浪過前洲
戲鷗掠水英姿俏　　騷客聯吟意興幽
綺麗江山呈眼底　　巍峨碉堡鎮山頭
拿翁昔日行軍過　　碉堡江山一併收

註：一、自布拉德斯拉瓦(Bratislava)乘遊艇沿多瑙河至
　　　　帝紋碉堡(Devin Castle)。
　　二、拿翁：拿破崙。帝紋古堡，部份為拿破崙軍隊所
　　　　燬。

摩拉維亞山區石窟(Moravian Caves)

萬年山嶽聳天空　　鬼斧神工顯洞中
石筍石鬚懸峭壁　　玉人玉馬踏尖峰
雲梯曲折人能上　　溪水縱橫舟可通
如此景觀何處覓　　摩山石窟寄遊蹤

註：摩拉維亞石窟在捷克的布爾諾(Brno)城郊外。

布拉格(捷克首都)

歷代帝王曾虎踞　　都城建築美無倫
教堂尖塔高高立　　碉堡雄姿處處陳
碎石長街思古意　　綠蔭紅瓦喜清新
每回幸免烽煙劫　　想是上蒼分外珍

註：捷克首都布拉格(Prague)為歐州最美之城市，尤以建
　　築著稱。各時期之建築風格，在此均有代表。在兩次
　　世界大戰中，此城因不在戰略要點，故未遭破壞。

華沙(波蘭首都)

左右強鄰如虎豹　　國家幾度遭瓜分
鐵蹄踐踏仍無懼　　抗暴英名舉世聞

奧斯維欽(Oswiecim)前德軍集中營遺址所見

四百萬條生命絕　　遺留頭髮如山積
希魔暴虐勝秦皇　　一心要把猶民滅

註：一、奧斯維欽在波蘭南部，為第二次世界大戰中德
　　　　軍毒殺四百餘萬猶太人所在地。
　　二、希魔：希特勒。
　　三、猶民：猶太民族。

布達佩斯(匈牙利首都)

羅馬帝國今安在　　匈奧王朝亦盡衰
歷代興亡千古事　　今來憑弔有餘哀

維也納(奧地利首都)

哈伯王朝陳眼前　　豪華宮殿憶當年
須知金碧輝煌裏　　都是平民血汗錢

註：哈伯王朝 Habsburg Dynasty

多瑙河(維也納段)

各國遊人滾滾來　　多瑙河畔且徘徊
古城美景留遺跡　　河水悠悠去不回

墨西哥阿克布可之旅

阿市鳥瞰

阿市稱良港　山城景色新
當年窩海盜　今日款詩人

註：阿克布可市（Acapulco）為墨西哥南部太
平洋旁之天然良港，現為渡假聖地。十
六世紀西班牙艦隊曾以此為基地，前往
東方淘寶。第十九屆世界詩人大會在此
舉行。

國際聯吟

各國文人會　聯吟共此時
登台賴番語　朗誦少陵詩

海灣日落

日沒光猶在　水天一片紅
遙知天盡處　旭日正當空

夜城拂曉

燈似星羅布　晶晶映水清
管絃聲不斷　徹夜到黎明

沙灘遠眺

雲彩天邊失　夕陽大海吞
沙灘留足印　潮去了無痕

懸崖策杖

前懸千仞壁　外望太平洋
策杖崖邊立　詩思萬里翔

愛琴海詩旅

2000 年 8 月，前往希臘，參加第二十屆世界詩人大會，並沿愛琴海，作探古之旅。

愛琴海

文化探源到愛琴　　追蹤歷史把根尋
遙聽海上風濤裏　　隱雜先民呼喚音

希　臘

文明進步賴交流　　學術巨人名永留
追溯源頭古希臘　　再經羅馬播全歐

雅典帕特儂神殿

神宮高聳數千年　　守護名城萬世傳
歷盡滄桑烽火劫　　猶存石柱鎮山巔

註：帕特儂 Parthenon 神殿供奉雅典守護神雅典那 Athena，
　　建於紀元前五世紀，全部用大理石建成，為世界最美
　　麗建築之一，現內部已燬，僅存週圍之石柱。

渡　海

渡輪海上御風行　　碧水藍天照眼明
遙想群雄爭霸處　　艨艟戰艦鬼神驚

古都塞薩洛尼基

希北古都旁愛琴　　廟堂城堡密如林
東羅帝國多遺跡　　過客徘徊感慨深

註：塞薩洛尼基 Thessaloniki 為希臘北部之古城，亞歷
　　山大大帝出生地，曾被羅馬征服。甚多寺廟城堡均
　　為拜占庭 Byzantine 王朝之建築。第二十屆世界詩
　　人大會在此召開。

詩人大會

異國騷人聚一堂　　你吟我唱意洋洋
重溫舊友迎新友　　身處他鄉似故鄉

註：世界詩人大會，由美國文化藝術學院主辦，每年在
　　不同之國家舉行。今年在希臘，出席詩人二百餘人，
　　來自三十三個國家。

薩摩斯島

薩摩小島產先賢　　伊索大名舉世傳
一冊寓言能解渴　　猶如荒漠湧甘泉

註：希臘外島薩摩斯 Samos，靠近土耳其海岸，為進入土
　　耳其國境之門戶。據傳「伊索寓言」之作者出生於此。

古特洛伊城

遠征特洛傷亡慘　　木馬屠城奏凱還
中外古今同一嘆　　十年殺戮為紅顏

註：特洛伊 Troy 為考古學家發現之古城，證明為荷馬史
　　詩中所描述之特洛人戰爭 Trojan War 所在地。在紀
　　元前 1184 年希臘人與特洛人在此作戰，長達十年。
　　據史詩中傳說，戰爭起因為爭奪當時希臘第一美人
　　海倫 Helen。

—14—

棉花堡

棉花堡底蓄溫泉　　堡號棉花不見棉
一片山岩如白玉　　要和雲彩競清妍

註：巴穆嘉麗 Pamukkale，土耳其地名，意譯為棉花堡。
　　因此一地區之山岩，雪白如棉花，由數千年來礦泉中
　　之鈣質，累積而成，蔚為奇觀。

石　棺

何事人生最可哀　　旅程短短去無回
石棺埋土千年在　　棺內皮囊早化灰

註：棉花堡附近，有一古墳場，甚多石棺出土，狀極淒涼。

伊斯坦堡

伊城雄踞三叉口　　戰略要衝跨亞歐
羅帝東都稱盛世　　遺留文物傲全球

註：伊斯坦堡 Istanbul 為土耳其北部橫跨歐亞兩洲之大
　　城。前為東羅馬帝國之首都，長達千餘年，遺留文物
　　甚豐。

夏威夷群島之旅

休閒聖地

天上白雲飄　　水邊棕樹搖
休閒何處去　　夏島遠塵囂

海邊遠眺

海風翻白浪　　雲雁點青天
遙望煙波裡　　巨鯨噴玉泉

大島(夏威夷本島)

大島島齡輕　　荒涼觸目驚
火山仍活躍　　時作不平鳴

註：島上尚有兩活火山口，仍不時爆發。

溶漿遺跡

岩漿遍地流　　綠野變荒丘
極目皆焦土　　身疑在月球

流漿夜景

山頭多裂口　　不斷冒溶漿
金色龍蛇舞　　蜿蜒奔海洋

卡曼哈曼哈大帝銅像

勇哉哈大帝　征戰得英名
立像頻招手　動人思古情

註：卡曼哈曼哈大帝 Kamehameha the Great
　　1758-1819，夏威夷原住民領袖。統一
　　群島，曾建立夏威夷聯合王國。在大島
　　與歐胡島均立有銅像。

遊侏羅紀公園

巡視侏羅紀　山高谷又深
恐龍今不見　留待夢中尋

註：侏羅紀公園，在歐胡島火奴魯魯市郊，
　　為著名恐龍影片 Jurassic Park 拍攝場
　　地。現已闢為公園，供人遊覽。

珍珠港　訪美艦
阿利桑那號紀念館

珠港遭偷襲　創傷記憶新
殘船留教訓　莫讓永沉淪

觀戰爭紀錄片

慘史今重現　不禁淚濕巾
當年曾目睹　生命化灰塵

劫後餘生

憶　往

憶昔從軍效國忠　　沙場馳騁逞英雄
征衣曾滴千山雨　　戎馬遍吹萬里風
老去應憐華髮白　　歸來猶惜戰袍紅
當年豪氣今安在　　浪跡天涯一跛翁

二、生活點滴

江南老兵

我本江南一老兵　　徘徊書劍兩無成
而今卸甲歸田隱　　桃李滿園享晚晴

當年投筆去從戎　　正是強鄰壓境中
只奈蕭牆烽火起　　贏來勝利竟成空

八年征戰走西川　　半世避秦台海邊
多少亂離多少苦　　為家為國兩難全

風雨無情歲月侵　　門前松柏自成蔭
何須成敗英雄論　　得失由來在寸心

窮　忙

請問先生何事忙　尋詩覓句索姑腸
詞貧難遣胸中意　一首吟成淚兩行

請問先生何事忙　家中瑣務一籮筐
縱然兒女都成長　尚有小孫尿我床

請問先生何事忙　天天親自下廚房
山珍海味都嘗遍　偏愛香菇豆腐湯

請問先生何事忙　朝勤做活夜收場
緣何終日無休歇　我本生來工作狂

還鄉探親(1991年)

去國流亡四十年　　生離死別恨綿綿
即今得遂還鄉願　　殘缺心情難補填

別後山河幾變遷　　歷經滄海又桑田
縱然路斷音書絕　　總有相思一線牽

隔洋西望霧濛濛　　多少鄉思入夢中
似海親情何處訴　　醒來總是一場空

半生戎馬走天涯　　夜夜追思歲月賒
四十年來空盼望　　而今歸去已無家

一路風塵兩鬢霜　　近鄉情怯淚盈眶
依稀往事猶堪憶　　只是音容已渺茫

故園細認舊時痕　睹物思親欲斷魂
昔日叮嚀猶在耳　只今侍奉已無門

百劫歸來獨此身　滿腔幽憤與誰申
親朋相對同聲哭　歷盡風霜剩幾人

全城寺廟遭文革　暮鼓晨鐘不再敲
莫問兒時遊樂處　斷牆殘瓦鬼神號

街頭巷尾鬧啾啾　小鎮風光不復留
好景已無西白漾　休閒空有目瀾洲

註：西白漾與目瀾洲為我家鄉盛澤鎮之風景點，現西白漾
　　已填為陸地，建立工廠。

如煙似夢憶當年　物換星移景色遷
安得春風吹大地　撥開雲霧見清天

跌傷自嘲

撲通跌一跤　股骨痛難熬
急急進醫院　撿還命一條

倒下難爬起　一肢已折離
剖開換關節　醫學顯神奇

手執龍頭杖　步行上下顛
猶如鐵栯李　跛足亦神仙

註：1994 年 7 月，股骨跌傷。

素食頌

可口芝麻餅　清心豆腐湯
雞魚雖美味　那及菜根香

蔬果天天吃　維生樣樣齊
健康無秘訣　素食最相宜

無事莫高歌　禍從口出多
如何消此劫　吃素唸彌陀

病榻囈語

無端又被機車撞　　換得小休病榻眠
可嘆人間多惱事　　養神閉目學參禪

人生底事受熬煎　　病痛傷殘豈偶然
骨折上膏何足道　　無邊苦海更堪憐

人體復元賴補充　　蜘蛛結網候飛蟲
求生意念原無異　　都在耐心等待中

老來筋骨漸疏鬆　　夢想求師學武功
安得名家來指點　　金剛練就顯神通

窗前花鳥正喧譁　　勾起遊情空自嗟
且待傷痊重出發　　再尋詩夢闖天涯

註：2000 年 6 月，遭機車撞傷，臥榻月餘。

歲月催人

七五感懷

忙忙亂世身　碌碌走紅塵
枉讀三千卷　虛拋七五春
孤鴻悲落寞　老馬忍艱辛
吟嘯烽煙裏　知音有幾人

八十自嘲

莫笑龍鍾態　我今已八旬
箋函遲作覆　書卷早生塵
聽曲迎風賞　觀花隔霧尋
出門誰與伴　手杖不離身

八五自誇

人海一舟浮　匆匆八五秋
遨遊償宿願　吟唱遣新愁
鐵腕攀三峽　鋼肢跨五洲
何來機器客　不倒不言休

註：余手足跌傷，裝有鐵片鐵釘，有如機器
人。

修爲三章

爲　人

爲人要至誠　　虛僞最傷情
有愛親朋睦　　無貪理義明
遇危應互助　　見利莫相爭
不作違心事　　坦然過一生

爲　學

爲學在於勤　　求知惜秒分
啟航先定向　　循序自成文
博覽窮根柢　　遨遊廣見聞
何來花與果　　不斷苦耕耘

爲　政

爲政在英明　　中庸未必行
是非應辨白　　利弊要分清
謀取全民福　　調和派系爭
何須成敗計　　歷史有公評

三、景物觀感

迎千禧年

時若舟航一葉輕　　無休無歇向前行
歷朝興替雲煙過　　萬種創傷歲月平
且慢回頭悲逝水　　應先額手慶新生
漫長黑夜終將盡　　千道霞光照眼明

晚　景

閱盡風霜看夕陽　　海天空闊滿紅光
功名幻影全消逝　　富貴浮雲已隱藏
眼見彩霞頻照耀　　心隨靈雀任飛翔
逍遙世外無牽掛　　不枉南山走一場

寶　島

太平洋上水連天　　屹立西南一島懸
百鳥爭鳴通款曲　　群花齊放競新妍
縱橫阡陌龍蛇舞　　遠近山河錦繡牽
莫道人間無樂土　　蓬萊仙境不虛傳

故宮博物院

莊嚴肅穆故宮牆　　雄峙雙溪大道旁
陳列藝文皆歷史　　搜羅寶物滿琳琅
前朝名畫高高掛　　絕世奇珍細細藏
此福從來天子享　　如今百姓亦能嘗

大漢溪

尋勝探幽枓崁西　　峰巒疊翠使人迷
溪名大漢懷先祖　　亭供觀音佑眾黎
靈塔斜陽風習習　　板山古道草萋萋
銘傳昔日屯兵地　　鴻爪依然留雪泥

921 大地震

地牛何事亂翻身　震得災黎哭鬼神
最是高樓傾塌處　成千生命付灰塵

家破人亡不忍觀　禍從天降起無端
縱然救出生還者　心受創傷肢已殘

搶救活埋成效微　幼童僥倖獲生機
可憐父母雙罹難　留下孤兒何處依

各方馳援見精神　捐款獻糧不後人
十萬災民無處宿　帳篷架起暫棲身

住屋已成瓦礫場　前瞻後顧兩茫茫
誰知一夕風雲變　重建家園道路長

註：1999 年 9 月 21 日晨，台灣中部發生強烈地震，傷亡
　　慘重。

辛巳重九感賦（2000 年）

轉瞬又重陽　詩人過節忙
登高舉目望　不禁淚涕滂
土石出山谷　衝倒房和屋
親人遭活埋　災民伏地哭
家庭竟失常　逆子殺爹娘
夫妻互相砍　幼兒亦遭殃
時逢不景氣　生活無以繼
掀起自殺風　放棄柴與米
亦有不甘休　冒險搶或偷
電眼全都錄　終作階下囚
哀哉千禧年　帶來千種禍
請問老天爺　究竟誰之過

書中田園

摩詰文章畫意深　　淵明詩句現山林
書中亦有田園趣　　何必出門遠處尋

小園春意

小園春意正欣欣　　鬆土栽花不厭勤
收獲幾多君莫問　　人生樂趣在耕耘

隱　者

興來忙裏且偷閒　　信步街頭獨往還
名利拋開心自得　　隱居何必覓深山

清　明

濛濛細雨又清明　　燒紙焚香觸目驚
遙念親恩猶未報　　人天永隔恨難平

七　夕

新月高懸映碧波　　牛郎織女會銀河
莫嫌天上良宵短　　應惜人間怨偶多

中　秋

應是團圓歡樂時　　忍看兒女又奔馳
無情最是中秋月　　不管人間有別離

辭　歲

滾滾紅塵裏　匆匆又一年
換時更日曆　送歲誦詩篇
正惜青春逝　忽驚白髮添
前程尚有約　路遠待加鞭

迎　新

闖入時光道　又逢歲月交
迎新多爆竹　送禮盡紅包
鑼鼓喧天響　彩花滿地拋
回頭已無路　惟有向前跑

朝　氣

旭日正東昇　清晨萬象興
園中花怒放　樹上鳥翻騰
豪氣隨風起　壯懷似霧蒸
欲酬千里志　振翼效飛鵬

春　曉

朝霞紅滿山　　溫暖到人間
美女睜迷眼　　俊男展笑顏
枝頭聲唧唧　　溪畔水潺潺
萬物皆蘇醒　　春風度玉關

郊　遊

郊外天空闊　　鄉間景色鮮
和風梳麥浪　　細雨潤瓜田
鳥語清而脆　　菜花香且妍
人間有佳境　　不復羨神仙

西湖遇雨

遙望西湖景　　茫茫一片空
堤傍聲寂寂　　湖上雨濛濛
畫舫淒迷裏　　亭台隱約中
淡濃均不見　　雲霧藏仙蹤

註：蘇東坡以西湖比西子，有「淡妝濃抹總
　　相宜」之句。

詠物三章

殘　燭

閃鑠西窗下　影搖百態生
光寒心內熾　腰細掌中輕
歷受風塵劫　那堪露水情
更殘人入夢　垂淚到天明

老　松

崢嶸一古松　屹立半山中
張臂迎雛雀　挺身抗勁風
徒悲皮剝落　無奈骨疏鬆
猶有傲霜志　心餘力不從

路　燈

出世落風塵　街頭寄此身
整天昏若醉　徹夜醒如神
嚇阻牽羊手　照明失路人
孤高空自賞　默默數酸辛

四、社會百態

偷拍歪風

更衣密室試新裝　　對鏡弄姿細品量
針眼偷窺留艷影　　打開網路洩春光

西風東漸

忽見滿街狐狸精　　朱脣赤髮正流行
西風吹動群芳舞　　自古效顰留笑名

檳榔西施

從來美女愛梳妝　　今日西施著泳裝
露臂袒胸三角褲　　沿街奔走送檳榔

狗仔隊

街頭巷尾語紛紜　狗仔跟蹤不厭勤
偵得名人婚外戀　全城媒體炒緋聞

金光黨

金光無處不張羅　老婦老翁受騙多
只為貪心投陷阱　一生積蓄付滄波

仙人跳

雲雨巫山興正濃　忽聽門外響咚咚
原來一齣仙人跳　嚇得情郎無地容

情人節

結彩張燈何事忙　卡拉歌唱正開場
今宵歡渡情人節　辣妹帥哥徹夜狂

娼妓文化

艷幟全球到處揚　　燈紅酒綠喜洋洋
古來多少營銷業　　賣笑行當最久長

桃色風波

財色糾纏亂若絲　　笑看主角盡愚痴
情仇恩怨何從起　　都是庸人自擾之

老少配

姻緣本是由天定　　莫笑少夫配老妻
燭影搖紅羅帳裏　　一頭婆鴨伴童雞

金　權

權勢金錢佔上風　　公平正義竟成空
鋤奸除惡人稱快　　只是流行小說中

度假外交

府衙枯坐太無聊　　度假放洋辦外交
名位稱呼全不計　　高球場上且逍遙

選　舉

滿街車隊鬧喧喧　　彷彿有人中狀元
一馬當先雙手拱　　聲聲拜託請支援

謾罵政治

議壇爭吵弄權謀　　政客罵人為出頭
神聖殿堂被污染　　選民掩臉盡蒙羞

股　市

股票市場似賭場　　翻紅翻黑變無常
縱然贏得千千萬　　一旦落空盡泡湯

樂透彩券

問卜求神好運尋　明牌暗碼注多金
到頭錢落他人袋　樂透悲來淚滿襟

行路難

機車攤販當街擺　路上行人擠又推
巴士疾馳忙閃躲　幾番慶幸得生回

環境污染

車噴廢氣塞天空　廠洩污流滲土中
環保設施如有失　禍延後代患無窮

義工溫情

不辭勞累助孤零　貧病無依得救星
莫道人間多冷酷　義工到處有溫馨

附錄

參加歷屆世界詩人大會講詞及詩

1. Introducing the Chinese Short Verse

2. War and Peace in Chinese Poetry

3. Poetry and Art

4. Poems

Presented at
The 18th World Congress of Poets
August 15-23, 1998
Bratislava, Slovakia

Introducing
the Chinese Short Verse
中國絕詩簡介

by J. S. Soong
宋哲生

Poets Meet in Bratislava

On the occasion of
the 18th World Congress of Poets

From all lands poets are gathered in the hall,
Disposed to search for poems, one and all.
Their poignant lines are sure to last forever
And cheer the hearts of people wheresoever.

To keep out evil, peaceful songs they sing
And warm up friendly talks with wine they bring.
This meeting in Brati gives a shining sight
And makes the mighty Danube burning bright.

J. S. Soong

詩人會布城　宋哲生

寰宇騷人聚一堂
撚鬚搔首索詩腸
吟來警句傳千古
譜出佳音娛四方
齊唱和平驅戾氣
互通心曲飲瓊漿
布城雅集空前事
多瑙河邊萬丈光

Introducing the Chinese Short Verse

The Chinese short verse is one of the most popular forms of expression in the Chinese literature. It developed early in history, flourished all the time while other poetic forms were blooming and fading, and has remained a favored form of expression until this day.

Why, then, is it so popular?

First of all, its compact form consisting of four lines of equal length with either 5 or 7 monosyllabic words each, allows only simple language, leaving little room for ornamentation. This quality of simplicity makes the Chinese short verse easily accessible to everyone.

In the following poem, the famous T'ang poet Li Po (701-762) uses everyday language to relate an experience, which may be shared by anyone being away from home.

> The moonlight shines before my bed,
> Like hoarfrost lying on the ground.
> To trace the moon I raise my head
> And then turn down, thoughts homeward bound.

低頭思故鄉　舉頭望明月　疑是地上霜　床前明月光　夜思　李白（唐）

Secondly, the Chinese short verse is intended to be
read aloud or sung. Like its English equivalent, it
follows certain patterns of rhythmical and rhyming ar-
rangement. In the four short and plainly worded lines,
alliteration and internal rhyming are also used to please
the ear as well as stress a point. All these musical
devices enable the Chinese short verse to be delightfully
carried from mouth to mouth and through generation after
generation.

Here is an example of its musical charm in a poem
entitled The Weaving Woman by Ch'u Mo, a poet in the 9th
century:

Behind the thatched door moans a thatch-haired maid.
A small light by her weaves she all night long.
When the brocade is made and taxes paid,
Her toil's not even worth a singer's song.

織婦　　處默（唐）

蓬鬢蓮門積恨多
夜來燈下不停梭
成縑猶自陪錢納
未直青樓一曲歌

Thirdly, the Chinese short verse is a versatile form that can be readily used to express any kind of ideas and feelings. It can tell a story, paint a scene, release emotions, give instructions, or satirize injustices. Very often it may carry hidden messages between the lines. The following examples may show a few of its various uses.

Here is one, in which a languishing wife complains about her suffering:

Much has changed since the day you took your leave;
No longer sit I on the loom to weave.
In thinking of you, I'm like a full moon, bright
But getting thinner, paler every night.

Chang Chiu-ling (673-740)

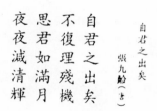

自君之出矣　張九齡（唐）

夜　不　思　自
夜　復　君　君
減　理　如　之
清　殘　滿　出
輝　機　月　矣

Here is another that satirizes superficial literary criticism:

Original thought sprouts from one's own views,
But loose expressions in art circles flow.
How can a dwarf in theater see the show?
Along with audience he applauds and boos.

Chao Yi (1723-1814)

—47—

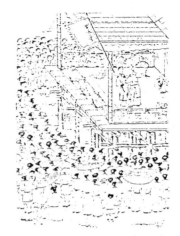

論詩　趙翼（清）

隻眼須憑自主張
紛紛藝苑說雌黃
矮人看戲何曾見
都是隨人說短長

Here a short verse narrates what is happening in a
morning. At the first reading, it sounds innocent enough,
but a second reading would reveal that the poem was written
after a war, in which many young men had been killed.

Still sleepy, of daybreak I'm not aware.
But listen! Birds are singing everywhere.
Last night, amid the splash of wind and rain,
How many budding flowers must've been slain?
                    Meng Hao-jan (689-740)

春曉　孟浩然（唐）

春眠不覺曉
處處聞啼鳥
夜來風雨聲
花落知多少

Another short verse describes a singing thrush, im-
plicitly hinting at freedom of speech:

> A thousand varying tones, at will they flush and flow
> In flowers pink and purple, in trees high and low.
> The thrush, I now find, locked up in a golden cage
> Can't sing as merrily as in its hermitage.
>
> Ou-yang Hsiu (1007-1072)

不山始山百
及花知花嘲
林紅鎖紅千
間紫向紫聲
自樹金樹隨
在高籠高意
啼低聽低移

畫眉鳥

歐陽修（宋）

Still another is didactic, offering advice to enjoy
life while one is still young:

> Care not the fine robe wov'n with threads of gold;
> Care but the precious moments in your prime.
> So, pluck the flowers while their buds unfold,
> Lest you have only empty branches to climb.
>
> Tu Ch'iu-niang (9th century)

金縷衣　杜秋娘（唐）

勸君莫惜金縷衣
勸君惜取少年時
花開堪折直須折
莫待無花空折枝

To sum up, the Chinese short verse, with its simple language, musical sound, and versatile functions, is a poetic form most widely used and loved. It can be seen everywhere, not only in books and pictures but also on the walls of temples and teahouses. As a result, it has survived many other poetic forms during the past fifteen hundred years and probably will continue to prevail throughout the next millennium.

In closing, the writer wishes to present a short verse of his own as follows:

An Old Poet

When young, on horse he rode
    Out on the battlefield.
While getting older, he taught
    And in learned circles wheeled.
Now white haired, out of tune,
    Refusing to keep dumb,
But singing under the moon,
    A poet has he become.

詩翁　宋哲生

青春躍馬沙場上
壯歲傳經學苑中
可笑白頭無所事
吟風弄月作詩翁

Presented at
the 19th World Congress of Poets
October 25-29, 1999
Acapulco, Mexico

War and Peace
in
Chinese Poetry

By J. S. Soong

War and Peace in Chinese Poetry

It is a pleasure, as well as a priviege, for me to
be here attending this 19th World Congress of Poets. We
are all lovers of poetry. The motto of the Congress is
"World peace through poetry." So, here we have a common
goal. But one would ask: What a poet can do to promote
peace of the world?

One way he can do it is to tell the world, through
his poetic works, how he thinks or feels about war and
peace. But the trouble is that there is the language
barrier. Should I speak in Chinese, few people here could
understand me. So, what I am trying to do today is to
to read some Chinese poems, in English of course, about
war and peace. This, I hope, may help in furthering mutual
understanding between poets of different countries.

In the long history of China, there have been more
years of war than years of peace. Naturally, the Chinese
people are weary of wars. Only on occasions of fighting
against foreign invaders may war heroes be exalted in poetry.
The general feeling toward war is one of repugnance as
reflected in the following poems.

First, I am going to read a warrior's farewell song:

A Warrior's Farewell Song

The soldier sadly tells his wife
That he may not return alive.
"To sooth my soul that lies beneath,
Take care of our dear baby please."

The wife, replying, heaves a sigh:
"A man should for his country die.
When unto border dust you drop,
A stone I'll be on the mountaintop."

Liu Chi (15th century)
Translated by J. S. Soong

—53—

A stone on the mountaintop refers to a story about a
faithful wife who turns into a stone on a mountaintop
after many years of watching in vain for the return of
her husband from war.

The next poem I will read is a protest against war-
mongers:

In the Year of War

The land of hills and lakes is torn by civil strife,
And people can no longer live a peaceful life.
Talk not of winning noble names in prideful tones;
A general's fame is built on countless human bones.

Ts'ao Sung (9th century)
Translated by J. S. Soong

The most pathetic description of the scenes from war
is found in a Song of War-chariots by Tu Fu, one of the
greatest poets in Chinese history. Here it is:

A Song of War-chariots

The war-chariots rattle,
The war-horses whinny.
Each man of you has a bow and a quiver at his belt.
Father, mother, son, wife, stare at you going,
Till dust shall've buried the bridge beyond Ch'ang-an.
They run with you, crying, they tug at your sleeves,
And the sound of their sorrow goes up to the clouds;
And every time a bystander asks you a question,
You can only say to him that you have to go.
...We remember others at fifteen sent north
   to guard the river
And at forty sent west to cultivate the camp-farms.
The mayor wound their turbans for them when they
   started out.
With their turbaned hair white now, they are still at the
   border,
At the border where the blood of men spills like the sea--
And still the heart of the emperor is beating for war.
...Do you know that, east of China's mountains,
   in two hundred districts
And in thousands of villages, nothing grows but weeds,
And though strong women have bent to the ploughing,
East and west the furrows all are broken down?
...Men of China are able to face the stiffest battle,
But their officers drive them like chickens and dogs.
        Whatever is asked of them,
        Dare they complain?
        For example, this winter
        Held west of the gate,
        Challenged for taxes,
        How could they pay?

...We have learned that to have a son is bad luck--
It is very much better to have a daughter
Who can marry and live in the house of a neighbor,
While under the grass we bury our boys.
...Go to the Blue Sea, look along the shore
At all the old white bones forsaken--
New ghosts are wailing there now with the old,
Loudest in the dark sky of a stormy night.

By Tu Fu (712-770)
Translated by Witter Bynner

These are the sorrowful scenes from war in the old
times. In this nuclear age today, war would be much more
destructive and cause much greater sorrow than ever before.
Should a third world war ever come, that would mean the
end of the world.

Now, let us turn to the scenes of peace. I will also
read a few poems to show how ordinary people enjoy a
peaceful life.

Here is an old man taking a walk on a day in spring:

A Spring Day

By noon when wind turns mild and cloud looks thin,

I walk through flowers and willows to the lake.

People, not knowing the joyful mood I'm in,

Would say a young man's style I'm trying to fake.

Ch'eng Hao (1032-1085)
Translated by J. S. Soong

Here is a farmer enjoying his happy life in a
peaceful world:

The Happy Farmer

I have a hundred mulberry trees
    And seven acres of grain,
Providing sufficient food and clothes,
    And friends to entertain.

My goodwife comes with smiling face
    To welcome all our guests;
My children run with willing feet
    To carry my behests.

When work is done and evening come,
    We saunter to the park,
And there, 'neath elm and willow trees
    We're blithe as soaring lark.

With wine and song the hours fly by
    Till each in cloudland roams,
And then, content with all the world,
    We wander to our homes.

                By Ch'u Kuang-hsi (8th century)
                Translated by Charles Budd

Finally, I shall conclude my reading with a short
poem of my own, specially written for this occasion.

Poets Meet in Acapulco, Mexico

On the occasion of
the 19th World Congress of Poets
October 25-29, 1999

From many countries poets are here
Converged on this Pacific shore.
They're summoned to meet each year,
Their roles in poetry to explore.

Through all seas fruitful currents flow,
Spreading seeds of peace around the world.
Together poets work hard to plow
And would not rest till flowers unfurld.

By J. S. Soong

不　同　和　文　邊　一　太　世　　　　詩
見　心　平　藝　飲　年　平　界　　　　人
花　協　種　清　邊　一　洋　詩　　　　大
開　力　子　流　吟　度　畔　人　市夕開　會
誓　勤　佈　通　共　群　說　聚　　　　　　　第
不　耕　全　四　唱　英　從　美　日在墨西哥之阿克布可　十九屆世界詩人大會　宋哲生
休　墾　球　海　酬　集　頭　洲　於一九九九年十月二五日至二十九

—58—

Presented at
the 20th World Congress of Poets
August 15-20, 2000
Thessaloniki, Greece

Poetry and Art

by J. S. Soong
宋哲生

Poetry and Art

Poetry is closely related to other forms of art, particularly painting. We often experience some poetic feeling, while looking at a picture, or visualize a picturesque scene, as we read a poem. Therefore, it ia a common practice for a Chinese artist to accompany his picture with a poem or vice versa, for words and pictures may complement each other, making both more comprehensible and, consequently, more enjoyable.

Here I wish to give some samples to illustrate my point.

Following is a picture painted inside a shell, showing an old man on a bridge surrounded by willow trees. He is looking at the lake as if in search of something. What is he thinking or feeling? The artist gives his answer in a poem.

The original poem
in Chinese

題畫　佗保生（明）

淺碧湖頭水
輕颭柳外風
興來橋上立
詩思有無中

A Painted Scene

The lake weeds paint the water green,
A light wind washes the willows clean,
While musing on the bridge, I seem
To feel a poem afloat downstream.

Next is a poem describing wind with pictures so
that you can see the power of wind.

Wind

Empowered to blow down autumn leaves,
And bring forth flowers that spring conceives.
And push up waves a thous'nd feet high,
And bid bamboos forever slanted lie.

Li Chiao (644-713)

風　李嶠（唐）

解落三秋葉
能開二月花
過江千尺浪
入竹萬年斜

THE POWER OF WIND

Here is a picture of the setting sun on tidal waves with a stork flying over the water. So the poem reads:

A View of the Setting Sun
Whereto the flying bird is getting?
Upon the puffs of wind it flaps and flips.
The sun is half way down in setting;
Suddenly, into swirling waves it dips.

Kuo Lin (1767-1831)

登吳山望江 郭麐（清）

忽夕翼飛
墮陽然鳥
亂方乘欲
流在遠何
中半風去

Here is another picture showing three young ladies in a kitchen. What are they doing? The poem will tell you.

A Bride's Song
The third day sees the young bride kitchen-bound.
Hands cleaned, she brews a stew with meat chops ground.
Not knowing her mother-in-law's accostomed thirst,
She asks her sisters-in-law to taste it first.

Wang Chien (765-830)

新嫁娘詞 王建（唐）

先未洗三
遣諳手日
小姑作入
姑食羹廚
嘗性湯下

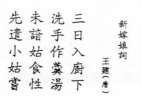

—63—

Finally, I will read a short poem of my own,
discribing a view of the Great Wall in China on a
photo of the Wall. As you may recall, when the
American astronaut Neil A. Armstrong landed on the
moon in 1969, he said that the Great Wall was the
only man-made object on earth that could be seen
from the moon. Following is the photo with the
poem.

長城遠眺　宋哲生

蜿蜒山嶽一條龍　拱衛邊疆挫敵鋒

首尾挺伸超萬里　月宮遙望見真容

A View of the Great Wall

A dragon winds through mountain ridges alone;
To guard the borders, never does it fail.
Stretched fifteen hundred miles from head to tail,
Its true looks only can be seen from the moon.

By J. S. SOONG

Presented at
XXI World Congress of Poets
7-11 October 2001
Sydney, Australia

Poems

by J. S. Soong
宋哲生

Australia, the Land of Peace and Poetry

In the southern hemisphere there lies a continent,
on whose soil never a war has been fought.
The gentle waves of the Pacific wash her shores;
a temperate climate prevails over her land.

Chewing leaves on trees are playful koalas,
the real Teddy bears that all children like.
Hopping in groups are lovely kangaroos,
who nourish their babies in abdominal pouches.

A poet cannot but be inspired and gay,
while taking a leisurely walk in bushes,
or viewing the sun-splashed harbour on waterfront,
or meeting the Three Sisters in the Blue Mountains.

Here, in a harmonious way, a new culture of pluralism
is developing among people of different origins.
The millennium, a hoped for period of peace and joy
foretold in the Book, is dawning on this continent.

A Song of Life

Life's like a candlelight
　　Seen flickering in the wind.
Though giving off heat and light,
　　It'll soon burn to an end.

Life's like a paper white;
　　Paint it red or green you might.
Too strong a shade's alarming;
　　A gentle touch more charming.

Life's like a cup of wine,
　　Sharing grief or joy of mine.
When savored as a treat,
　　I find it bittersweet.

Life's like a grain of sand
　　Drifting out to see the world.
But waves too fierce to stand;
　　Ambitious schemes all foiled.

Life's like a new-bloomed flower
　　With luster loved by all.
Forgotten when petals fall
　　Till next year's flowering hour.

Life's just a floating dream;
　　All riches fade like steam.
Those who discard vain strife
　　Shall live a happy life.

Note: The quoted poems and illustrations in the
above texts are taken from the book <u>Pearls in the
Shell</u>, a collection of best loved short verses from
the Chinese language, edited and translated by J. S.
Soong and published by Jain Publishing Company in
the United Statea. Anyone interested in the book
may contact the publisher directly at the following
address:
  Jain Publishing Company
  P. O. Box 3523
  Fremont, CA 94539
  U. S. A.
or: http://www.jainpub.com/

The book can also be ordered through all the major
internet booksellers such as Amazon.com (www.amazon.
com), Barnesandnoble.com (www.bn.com) and Borders.com
(www.borders.com).